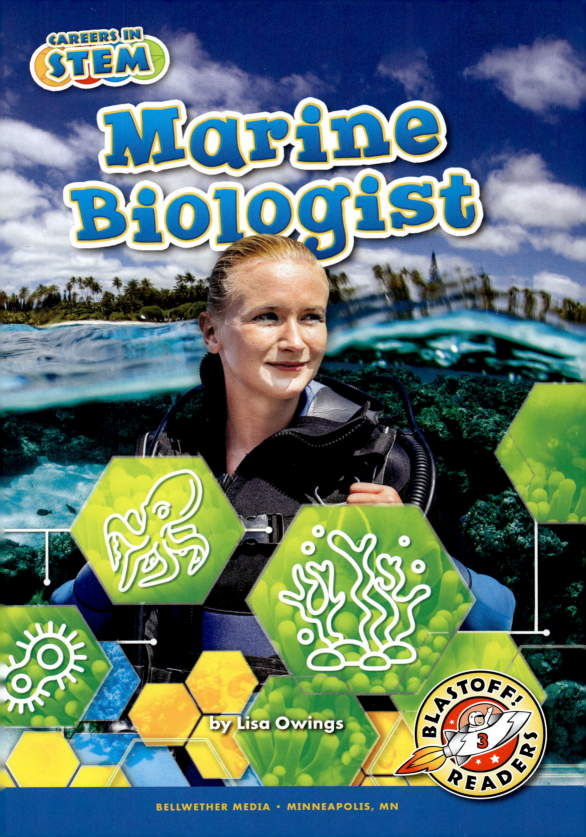

Blastoff! Readers are carefully developed by literacy experts to build reading stamina and move students toward fluency by combining standards-based content with developmentally appropriate text.

Level 1 provides the most support through repetition of high-frequency words, light text, predictable sentence patterns, and strong visual support.

Level 2 offers early readers a bit more challenge through varied sentences, increased text load, and text-supportive special features.

Level 3 advances early-fluent readers toward fluency through increased text load, less reliance on photos, advancing concepts, longer sentences, and more complex special features.

★ **Blastoff! Universe**

Reading Level: Grade K → Grades 1–3 → Grade 4

This edition first published in 2024 by Bellwether Media, Inc.

No part of this publication may be reproduced in whole or in part without written permission of the publisher. For information regarding permission, write to Bellwether Media, Inc., Attention: Permissions Department, 6012 Blue Circle Drive, Minnetonka, MN 55343.

Library of Congress Cataloging-in-Publication Data

LC record for Marine Biologist available at: https://lccn.loc.gov/2023001653

Text copyright © 2024 by Bellwether Media, Inc. BLASTOFF! READERS and associated logos are trademarks and/or registered trademarks of Bellwether Media, Inc.

Editor: Betsy Rathburn   Designer: Andrea Schneider

Printed in the United States of America, North Mankato, MN.

Table of Contents

A Deep Dive	4
What Is a Marine Biologist?	6
At Work	10
Becoming a Marine Biologist	16
Glossary	22
To Learn More	23
Index	24

A Deep Dive

A marine biologist looks out of a deep-sea **submersible**. He shines lights into the dark water.

Strange-looking fish swim past. He collects one. Later, he will study it in a **lab**!

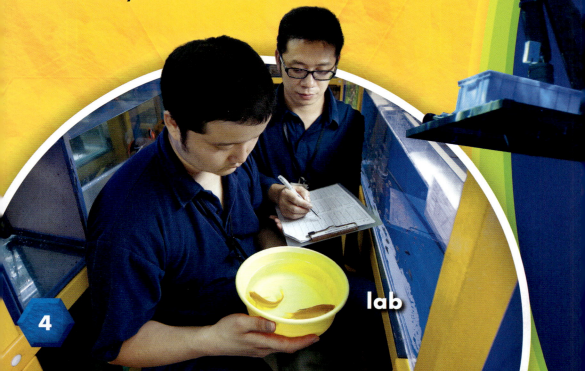

lab

deep-sea submersible

What Is a Marine Biologist?

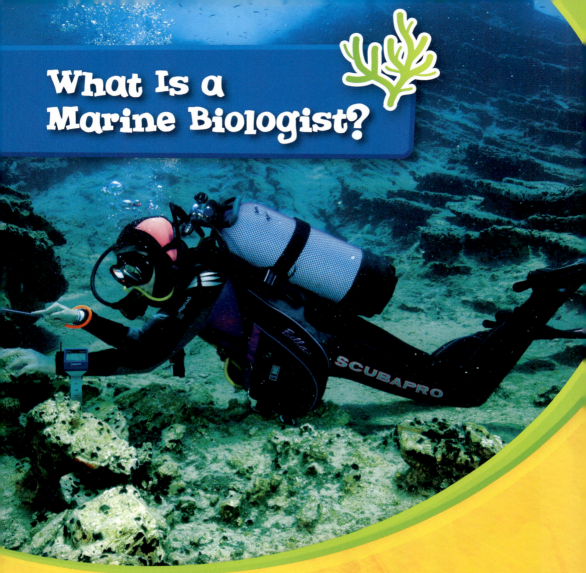

Marine biologists are scientists. They study ocean plants and animals. They study ocean **habitats**.

They work on boats or in the water. They take notes and collect **data**. They study their data in labs.

Marine Biology in Real Life

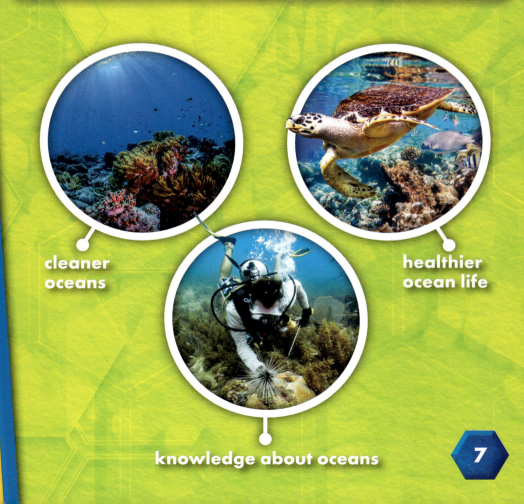

cleaner oceans

healthier ocean life

knowledge about oceans

They see how plants grow. They study harmful **algae blooms**. They watch what animals do. They follow where animals feed and travel.

Famous Marine Biologist

- **Name:** Eugenie Clark
- **Born:** May 4, 1922
- **Died:** February 25, 2015
- **Birthplace:** New York City, New York
- **Schooling:** Hunter College, New York University
- **Known For:** Studied sharks and taught people not to fear them

algae bloom

They study how humans affect oceans. Ocean health affects all life on Earth!

At Work

Marine biologists use tools to study ocean life. They **tag** animals and follow them with computers.

They use **satellites** to see the ocean from above. Robots let them reach deep waters.

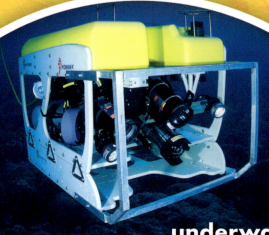
underwater robot

tagged sea turtle

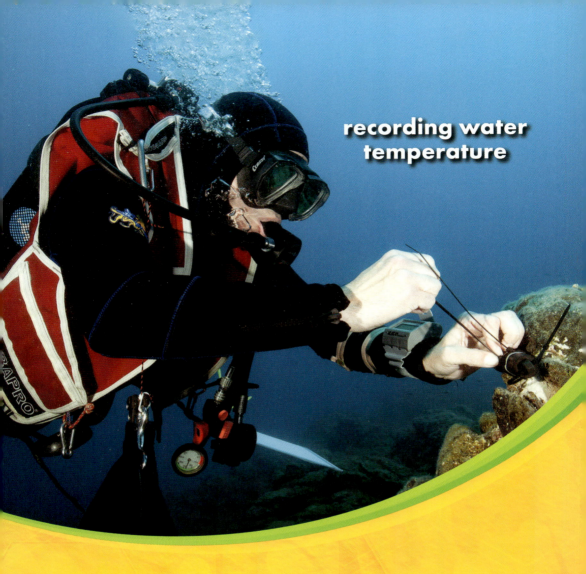

recording water temperature

They work to keep oceans healthy. Some study **climate change**. They watch how changes affect ocean life.

Others help control **pollution**. They study ocean trash and oil spills.

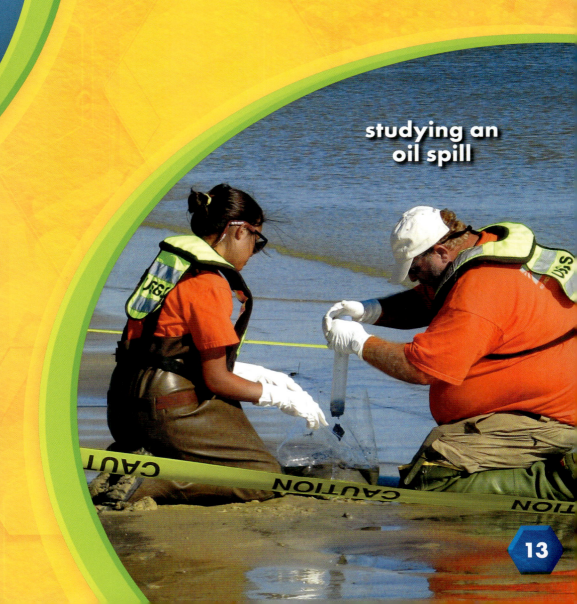

studying an oil spill

Ocean animals are an important food source for many people. But fishing can harm ocean habitats.

Using STEM

 Science — study ocean life

 Technology — use computers to collect data

 Engineering — create new tools to study ocean life

 Math — study patterns in data

restoring ocean habitat

Some marine biologists help **restore** ocean habitats. They help plants and animals grow!

Becoming a Marine Biologist

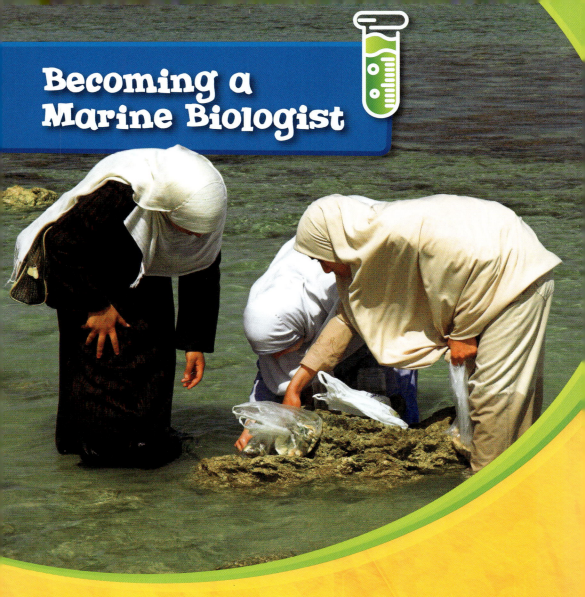

Most marine biologists go to college. They take math and science classes. They take lab classes.

Many go to **graduate school**. They choose a topic to study more closely.

Then, they find an **internship** or job. They help with someone else's **research**. They might work outdoors or in labs.

They grow their knowledge. They become better researchers. They get good at solving problems.

In time, they can lead their own projects. Some try to make new discoveries. Some write books or teach people.

How to Become a Marine Biologist

1. study math and science in college
2. study a topic further in graduate school
3. find an internship or job
4. lead projects

Their work helps people understand Earth's oceans!

Glossary

algae blooms—increases in the growth of algae in certain areas; algae are plants or plantlike living things.

climate change—a human-caused change in Earth's weather due to warming temperatures

data—information

graduate school—a school where people can study a specialty area after college

habitats—lands with certain types of plants, animals, and weather

internship—a position where a student can gain on-the-job experience

lab—a building or room with special tools to do science experiments and tests

pollution—something that is harmful to the air, water, or land

research—careful study to find new knowledge or information about something

restore—to repair something to make it like it originally was

satellites—human-made objects that circle Earth

submersible—a machine that can explore the deep sea

tag—to attach a device that allows scientists to collect information about animals

To Learn More

AT THE LIBRARY

French, Jess. *Earth's Incredible Oceans*. New York, N.Y.: DK Publishing, 2021.

Leaf, Christina. *Rachel Carson: Environmentalist*. Minneapolis, Minn.: Bellwether Media, 2019.

Nayak, Manisha. *I'm a Future Marine Biologist!* Hackensack, N.J.: WS Education, 2022.

ON THE WEB

FACTSURFER

Factsurfer.com gives you a safe, fun way to find more information.

1. Go to www.factsurfer.com.

2. Enter "marine biologist" into the search box and click 🔍.

3. Select your book cover to see a list of related content.

Index

algae blooms, 8, 9
animals, 6, 8, 10, 14, 15
Clark, Eugenie, 8
climate change, 12
college, 16
computers, 10
data, 7
graduate school, 17
habitats, 6, 14, 15
how to become, 20
humans, 9
internship, 18
lab, 4, 7, 16, 18
marine biology in real life, 7
math, 16
ocean, 6, 9, 10, 12, 14, 15, 21
oil spills, 13
plants, 6, 8, 15
pollution, 13
research, 18
restore, 15
robots, 10
satellites, 10
science, 16
submersible, 4, 5
tag, 10, 11
teach, 20
trash, 13
using STEM, 14

The images in this book are reproduced through the courtesy of: Anze Furlan, front cover (marine biologist); ethan daniels, front cover (background); beautiful scenery, p. 3 (jellyfish); mehmettorlak, p. 3 (coral reef); Billy Hustace/ Getty Images, p. 4 (lab); 1621855, pp. 4-5; zaferkizilkaya, pp. 6-7; Irina Markova, p. 7 (cleaner oceans); Andrey Armiagov, p. 7 (healthier ocean life); nicole helgasson, p. 7 (knowledge about oceans); Wikipedia, p. 8 (Eugenie Clark); Simon Pierce/ Alamy, pp. 8-9; smspsy, p. 9 (algae bloom); Porco_Rosso, p. 10 (underwater robot); David Fleetham/ Alamy, pp. 10-11; Images & Stories/ Alamy, pp. 12-13, 14-15; Shane J Stocks/ USGS, p. 13; Charles Stirling (Travel)/ Alamy, pp. 16-17; Steve Morgan/ Alamy, p. 17; Margus Vilbas Photography, p. 18; Cultura Creative RF/ Alamy, pp. 18-19; SolStock, pp. 20-21 (marine biologist); Bob Daemmrich/ Alamy, pp. 20-21; Richard Whitcombe, p. 23.

24